iPad Pro

OWNER'S MANUAL

Quick And Easy Ways to Master iPad Pro, iOS 12 and Troubleshoot Common Problems

John A Wilson

Copyright © 2018 by John A. Wilson- All rights reserved.

No part of this publication **iPad Pro Owner's Manual** may be reproduced, stored in a retrieval system or transmitted in any form or by any means, electronic, mechanical, photocopying, recording, and scanning without permission in writing by the author.

Contents

Introduction 1

How To Set Up The New iPad Pro 2

The USB-C Connector 11

How To Use The New iPad Gestures In iOS 12 17

How to Transfer Everything From Android Device to iPad Pro 22

Transfer Android data to iPad Pro via Move to iOS App 23

Transfer Android Data to iPad Pro using Syncios Data Transfer ... 28

Create an Apple ID 29

   How To Sign In To iCloud With An Existing Apple ID 32

   How To Sign Out Of iCloud On Your iPad 33

How To Set Up Mail, Contacts, And Calendars On iPad 34

How To Set Up Outlook.Com Mail, Calendar, And Contacts On iPad 35

   Setting Up Exchange Mail, Calendar, And Contacts On iPad 36

   How To Set Up IMAP/POP, Caldav, And Carddav On iPad 37

How To Adjust Display Zoom On iPad 38

How To Force Quit Apps On iPad Pro 39

How to Disable Apple Music Listening History On iPhone And iPad 40

Transfer Your Cellular Data Plan From Your Old iPad To Your New iPad 41

How To Transfer A Data Plan From One iPad With A SIM Card To Another 42

Use Your iPad Pro As A Display For Your Mac Mini 43

How To Take A Screenshot With The iPad Pro 46

How To Use Instant Markup For Screenshots 48

    How To Access Instant Markup 49

    How To Edit A Screenshot With Instant Markup 50

    How To Save An Edited Screenshot From Instant Markup ... 52

    How To Share An Edited Screenshot From Instant Markup . 53

    How To Disable Instant Markup 54

iPad Pencil 54

    Pair Your Apple Pencil With Your iPad 55

    How To Use Apple Pencil 56

    Charge Your Apple Pencil 59

How To Scan, Sign, And Send Documents 61

How To Create, Customize, And Use Memoji In iOS 12 62

Apple Pay 69

    How to Manage Apple Pay 70

    How to Use Wallet 70

How To Set up 'Hey Siri' on iPad 71

    How to Train "Hey Siri" to Your Voice..................................72

    How to Use "Hey Siri!" 73

    How Secure Is "Hey0Siri!" Voice ID?....................................73

Troubleshoot Common Problems..74

    iPad Pro shuts down or restarts by itself 75

    Echo in Skype calls and other video calls 76

    Can't connect to Wi-Fi...78

    Screen freezing during use 80

    Battery life is poor 83

    Smart Keyboard not working 85

    Unable to view and play videos 87

    Apple Pencil battery widget disappears...............................89

    No app or system sounds 90

Introduction

When the original iPad launched in 2010, it was in many ways a glorified iPhone with a significantly larger screen. That's not to say it wasn't an amazing product for the time — simply that you couldn't do a whole lot on it that wasn't already possible on Apple's smaller hardware. The idea of a responsive, stylus-free tablet was innovative enough, so things like multitasking support and flashy gesture controls would come much later.

Well, it's now 2018, and they have. Even if you're an iPhone X owner or a MacBook Pro devotee, the all-new iPad Pro is an entirely different beast. Sure, you could use it in much the same way you would an iPhone, but then you would be missing out on a plethora of shortcuts and tricks designed to better your experience. Thankfully, we assembled some of our favorite iPad Pro tips and tricks in this book, all of which will help you make the most of your device.

How To Set Up The New iPad Pro

Now it's time to get things set up! Thankfully, this is an easy process, especially if you already use an iPhone or iPad with iCloud.

There are a few things you need to do to move from your old iPad to a new one, or to migrate from an iPhone. And setting up a new iPad Pro from scratch isn't much harder — gone are the days of manually copying passwords just to get to the home screen.

Auto setup

Automatic Setup has been around since iOS 11, and is a fantastic feature. Just bring your old and new devices close to each other when prompted, and Automatic Setup will copy across your Apple ID and home Wi-Fi settings. It's like AirDrop, only with one very specific purpose.

It works like this, when you fire up your new iPad for the first time, any nearby iOS devices will detect it, and offer to do an Automatic Setup. The new device will show a dot-cloud pattern on its screen, and you use the camera of your old device to "scan" this like a QR code. Then you just follow along. Your iCloud login, Wi-Fi passwords, and everything else you need are transferred across. It's really amazing!

From there, you can either set up your iPad as a new device, or restore from a backup. One tip on restoring from backups is that you may prefer to use an iTunes backup instead of an iCloud backup. If you do this, be aware that it may take a lot longer. Also, make sure that you check the box in iTunes to encrypt your backups. This means that all you passwords will also be backed up and restored. Unencrypted back-ups don't include this sensitive information.

iTunes back-ups and restores can be dead slow. If you have a fast internet connection, an iCloud restore is much faster. If you don't, then an iTunes restore is the way to go.

Restore from backup

This is the hands-down the easiest way to move from an old iPad to a new one. All you have to do is make sure you have a recent backup from your existing iPad, and then point your new iPhone Pro at this iCloud backup. It will then download everything — all your settings, apps, passwords, even your wallpaper. When the process is done — and it could take a while depending on you internet speed, and the size of your backup — it'll be like you never left the old iPad. Even your Safari tabs will be intact.

Even if you never owned an iPad before, you can restore from a backup of your iPhone. That'll make it easier to get up and running, and you can always tweak things later.

To make a backup, head to the iCloud settings on your iPhone, and check that there is a recent automatic backup. If not, just do one manually. Head to **Settings > Your Name > iCloud > iCloud Backup** and tap **Back Up Now**. Wait until it's done.

Face ID

Next, you'll be prompted to set up Face ID. Face D is much easier to use than Touch ID, and it's also easier to set up. Instead of having to train your iPad with your fingerprints, one by one, you just look into the camera and… that's almost it. To set up Face ID on your iPad, just follow along when prompted during the initial setup. You'll have to hold the iPad up so its Face ID camera can see you, and then turn your head so it can scan your face. On-screen guides will show you how to place and move your head, and setup takes just a few moments. This is even more fun and science-fiction on the iPad, as the screen is so much bigger.

If you want to start over with Face ID setup, head to **Settings>Face ID & Passcode**, and tap in your password to get started. If you regularly sport a second appearance — you're a clown, a surgeon, an Elvis impersonator, or something similar, then you can also set up an alternate appearance. Just tap the button in the Face ID settings to set this up.

Apple Pencil

If you purchased an Apple Pencil along with your new iPad Pro, now is the time to set it up. And by "set it up," I really mean that you just take it out of its packaging and set it on the right edge of the iPad (when held "upright" in portrait mode). The magnets will snap it onto place, and the Pencil will pair and begin charging. You'll see a life-sized picture of the Pencil on screen to tell you it has happened. And that's it!

Add Apple Pay

Next up, add Apple Pay to your iPad. You'll be prompted to do this as part of the setup, but if you skip it, follow along here. Go to **Settings > Wallet & Apple Pay**. If you have previously added a credit or debit card to your Apple Pay account, you will have to re-activate it on this device. To do so, tap that card in the list (it will have **Unavailable** written below it), and follow the instructions. Procedures may differ depending on your bank. Then, if you like, you can set a default Apple Pay card.

Put apps and folders in the dock – optimize for drag-n-drop

Next up, get your apps sorted. The iPad Pro supports Apple's great drag-and-drop for apps. The iPad lets you drag apps from the Dock, and then drop them next to, or over, the current app, in order to use the split-screen view. Finding these apps is a lot easier if you keep them in folders in the Dock, because you can get to the Dock from inside any app by swiping up from the bottom of the screen. Which brings us to:

Consider a blank home screen

You might like to run your iPad with a blank home screen. It sounds radical, but I switched back in July and I'm still using it. The idea is that you keep the first home screen icon-free, and instead put all your most-used apps into a folder in the Dock. Then you can get instant access to all your favorite apps from anywhere in iOS, just by swiping up to reveal the Dock. It's almost essential for split-screen multitasking, but also great for everything else. Try it at least. You might love it

Switch on Dropbox in Files app

The new iPad Pro inherits all of iOS 12's flaws, but it still lets you use the powerful Files app. Open that up now and take a look at the left column in the Browse tab. This shows the various storage areas available to you — **iCloud Drive**, and On **My iPad**. The latter gives access only to the local storage folders created by apps — you can't actually create a folder in there. But you should tap the **Edit** button at the top of this list, and you'll see all the available sources. These are provided by third-party apps, and let you drop files into these apps, or to access their files, right inside the Files app.

For example, AudioShare is an amazing app for organizing your music files. It provides a Files folder, so you can use the AudioShare app to organize your music, but use the Files app to drag and drop that music onto other apps. This is also where you switch on Dropbox, and other cloud services.

Learn the gestures

Ever since iOS 12, the iPad has had iPhone X-like gestures. Even on the older iPad, with their home buttons and giant bezels, you can navigate without ever touching that home button. Swipes and taps can do everything. The good news is, if you are already used to the iPhone X or later, you will have nothing to learn. If you're new to iOS devices without home buttons, read "how to use the new iPad gestures in iOS 12."

Pick a name

This might be the hardest part of the setup. You'll need to pick a name for your new iPad Pro, one that you're happy with for the next few years. This name will show up on the network, it will be used to identify it in iCloud, and so on. I can't help you pick one — that's what baby and dog name books are for — but I can tell you how to change it. Go to **Settings > About**, and tap at the top of the list. Then just type in your new name, and you're done.

The USB-C Connector

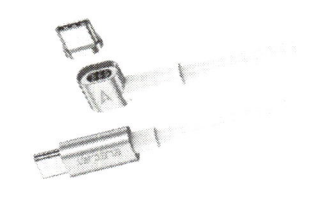

The USB-C connector will probably be more or less familiar to most tech fans. It's around the size of a Lightning connector, only it has a hole in the middle. It's also wobbly when plugged in. I hate it, but it brings some advantages, as we'll see.

Unlike other USB cables — Lightning, microUSB and so on — the USB-C cable is symmetrical. You can plug either end into either device. And the plug itself is also symmetrical, so you never try to shove it in upside-down.

The USB-C connector also looks just like the Thunderbolt 3 connector. That's because the USB-C spec calls for it to support additional functionality on top of its regular USB duties — Thunderbolt or DisplayPort, for example. This means that you can plug a Thunderbolt peripheral into a USB-C port, and it won't work. Or it might work a bit, but you might not get all the functions available if it were hooked up to a Thunderbolt 3 port. Oh, and you probably won't be able to tell the different between a USB-C and a Thunderbolt 3 cable.

In the case of the iPad Pro, though, USB-C means a few things. ==USB-C supports a lot more power than a Lightning cable — up to 100 watts.== That's why it can replace a 60-watt-plus MacBook charger.

It also appears that Apple is allowing the new iPad Pro to deliver more power outward, letting them power and charge connected peripherals like iPhones. Previously, the iPad could power connected accessories via Lightning, but more likely than not you'd get a warning that the accessory was drawing too much power. No longer! If you hook up a high-draw accessory, the iPad's battery will possibly drain even faster than before. To fix that, you'll need a powered hub.

What can you connect to iPad Pro via USB-C?

When it comes to connecting peripherals to iPad Pro via USB-C, the list of compatible devices is pretty much the same as it was with Lightning and the Lightning to USB 3.0 adapter. You can connect keyboards, audio interfaces, USB MIDI devices, Ethernet adapters, cameras and external storage (USB sticks and hard drives, but only for accessing photos and videos).

The new USB-C iPad Pro port doesn't add anything in terms of compatibility with other USB devices — it just changes the way you connect them. What you can't connect are old Lightning accessories. Anything that has a cable or plug that slips into the Lightning port is now dead to you, although perhaps you can find a new cable for it.

USB 3.1 gen 2

While the new iPad Pro connector is called USB-C, the stuff going through the wire has its own spec. Just like USB 2.0 and USB 3.0 shared a connector, USB-C specs can differ for the same plug. The iPad Pro uses the latest USB 3.1 gen 2, which can transfer data at up to 10 Gbps. Compare that to the USB 3.0 used in Lightning, with a maximum of 5 Gbps. While this makes little difference for most things (USB 2.0 is more than fast enough for music, for example), it is important for driving external 4K displays, and for hooking up many accessories to the iPad at once.

USB-C hubs

The iPad Pro's new USB-C port lets you connect USB-C device, obviously, but what does that mean exactly? Some current gadgets support USB-C, but often they ship with a USB-C to USB-A cable for connecting to PCs and older Macs. You can also only connect one accessory at a time, because the iPad Pro only has one USB-C port.

What you need is a USB-C hub. These are readily available thanks to the lack of ports on the MacBook. A hub will let you connect any number of accessories to your iPad. And thanks to that fast USB 3.1 gen 2 connection, there will be plenty of bandwidth for all.

USB-C hub essentials for iPad Pro

The important feature when it comes to USB-C hubs is pass-through power. Any old USB-C hub will let you connect accessories. But in order to power the iPad Pro at the same time, the hub should allow pass-through power. This lets you connect a charger to the hub. The hub will then pass that power on to the iPad, as well as (possibly) powering all those accessories.

The beauty of a USB-C hub is that you can have a permanent workstation on your desk and dock the iPad to it. A hub could be connected to power, an audio interface and speakers, musical instruments, an external display, a USB keyboard and also provide an SD card reader. That's pretty handy.

How To Use The New iPad Gestures In iOS 12

iOS 12 was clearly designed for an iPad where Face ID replaces the Home button. Apple has revamped the tablet's gestures for iOS 12, bringing us an easy way to return to the Home screen, and an iPhone X-style gesture to access the Control Center.

If you're a long-time iPad users, these changes will seem a little jarring at first. You'll soon get used to them, though, and even learn to love them. The new Control Center gesture, in fact, is a lot better than the old one.

iOS 12 iPad gestures

Which gestures have changed on iPad in iOS 12? In iOS 11, when you swipe up from the bottom of the screen, you first reveal the Dock (unless it is already visible), then keep on swiping up to access the Control Center. If you're hoping that this dual-purpose gesture has been simplified in iOS 12, you're out of luck. It has just been repurposed. The app-switcher gesture has kind of stayed the same, but currently, it's harder to use.

Same iOS gestures, different outcome

In iOS 12, the short swipe up still pulls up the Dock. However, when you keep swiping up, you now get returned to the Home screen. This seems to be Apple's plan for any future Face ID iPads that might lack a Home button.

The Control Center in iOS 12 gets a new home, and a new gesture. Control Center is now accessed the same way as on the iPhone X: You must swipe down from the top right corner of the screen. Do that, and the Control Center fades in, appearing in that same corner. To me, this is a much better gesture. It's shorter, for one, but it also leaves your finger over the Control Center's controls, which is where you want it to be.

Also, the Control Center is now active during a swipe. That is, you can swipe it into view, keeping that finger "active," and use another finger to quickly change the screen brightness (or tweak other things). Then you can swipe the Control Center back out of view. This is a very fast way to access controls.

The app switcher gesture in iOS 12

Where does this leave the iOS 12 app switcher? In iOS 11, Control Center and the app switcher shared the same screen. Swiping up from the bottom of the screen would bring up a sheet that showed both the Control Center and thumbnails of recently used apps.

Now, the app switcher is accessed by stopping short of the new Home screen swipe. You go past the Dock-drag, but you don't go as far as revealing the Home screen. In early beta versions, I found myself hitting the Home screen instead of the app switcher. In the final release, it's the other way around.

The iPad inherits another of those much-copied new iPhone X gestures as well. You can swipe up as if you're going to enter the full app switcher, but as soon as the current app starts to shrink onscreen, you can quickly swipe left or right to switch to the previous or next app. This is actually a fantastic gesture on the iPad.

If you are used to the four-or-five-finger swipe to move between apps, you'll love this one. It's exactly the same, only easier. It also works from the Home screen. And you can do it all with just one finger.

The old five-finger shuffle gets new tricks

Speaking of the five-finger gestures, these still work in iOS 12. You can use a four-or-five-finger swipe to switch apps, as mentioned above. This gesture also now works from the Home screen in iOS, letting you access your last-used app with a swipe. In iOS 11, using this gesture on the Home screen would just switch Home screen pages, or take you to the Today view — the same as using one finger. In iOS 12, it becomes a lot more useful.

The old four-or-five-fingered pinch also works to return you to the Home screen from an app, but you can now also use the same gesture to get to the app switcher. You do it like this:

First, pinch in on an app screen, but instead of pinching all the way to the Home screen, move your fingers left or right a little, and you'll see the app switcher come into view.

How to Transfer Everything From Android Device to iPad Pro

As Apple's iOS platform rises in popularity and challenges the Google Android's market share, more and more Samsung Galaxy Ta, Kindle Fire or Lenovo Yoga Tab users are intended to switch to the new iPad Pro with 12.9-inch Retina Display. Also, the Pencil is what moves the Pro into a completely different category than the other iPad.

If you were also one of Android tablet users and intended to buy a new iPad Pro, the first problem you should deal with is how to transfer all content from your Android tablet to iPad Pro. In order to solve this problem, we'll go over steps to move Android to iOS. There are two methods you can use to transfer data from an android device to iPad pro:

1. Transfer data to iPad Pro via **Move to iOS** App

2. Transfer Android data to iPad Pro using **Syncios Data Transfer**

Transfer Android data to iPad Pro via Move to iOS App

This is the best desktop backup app, one-click backup & recovery everything on Android. Move to iOS is Apple's new app that allows the Android users to move files of all types easily to iOS devices. This app will also match your paid apps found on the Android device against paid apps in the iOS. This app will automatically be added to you iTunes wish list. It requires iPhone or iPad on iOS 9 or later version, Android tablet on Android version 4.0 or later. You can download it on Google Play.

Before getting started, make sure that you have turned on Wi-Fi on your Android tablet, the content you're moving, including what's on your external Micro SD card, will fit on your new iOS device. Then, plug your new iOS device and your Android device in to power. If you want to transfer your Chrome bookmarks, you have to update to the latest version of Chrome on your Android device. follow these steps to transfer your data using Move To iOS:

1. While setting up your new iOS device, look for the Apps & Data screen. Then tap **Move Data from Android**. If you've already finished setup, you'll have to erase your iOS device and start over. If you don't want to erase, just transfer your content manually.

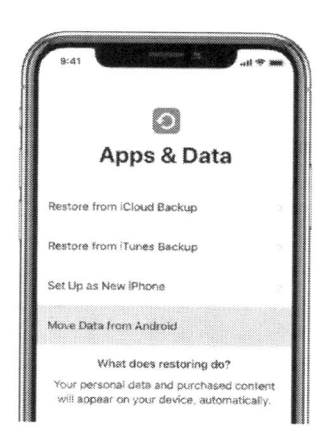

2. On your Android tablet, **open the Move to iOS app** and tap **Continue**. Read the terms and conditions that appear. Tap **Agree** to continue, then tap **Next** in the top-right corner of the Find Your Code screen.

3. On your iOS device, tap **Continue** on the screen called Move from Android. Then wait for a ten-digit code to appear.

If your Android device shows an alert that you have a weak Internet connection, you can ignore the alert. Then, Enter the code on your Android device. Then wait for the Transfer Data screen to appear.

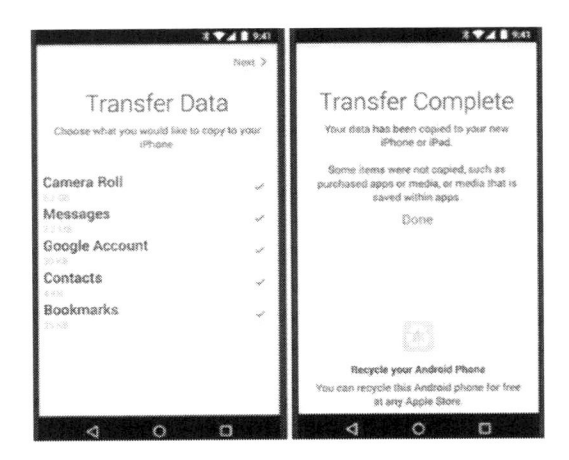

4. On your Android device, **select the content you'd like to transfer** and tap **Next**. Then leave both devices alone until the loading bar that appears on your iOS device finishes—even if your Android indicates that the process is complete. The whole transfer can take a while, depending on how much content you're moving.

5. After the loading bar finishes on your iOS device, tap **Done** on your Android device. Then tap **Continue** on your iOS device and follow the onscreen steps to finish setting it up.

After finished, navigate to your iPad Pro to make sure that all of your content transferred. If some didn't, you can move that content manually. Then go to the App Store on your iOS device to find and download apps that were on your Android device.

Transfer Android Data to iPad Pro using Syncios Data Transfer

Syncios Data transfer is a cross-platform data transfer, backup and restore assistant, available for both iOS and Android devices. It allows you to backup more than 12 types of phone data, including SMS, call logs, contacts, photos, videos, ebooks, apps, music, calendars etc on one click. Follow these steps:

1. **Install and run Syncios Data Transfer program**. Connect both of your iPad Pro and Android tablet to computer or Mac. Click **Start** button to start transferring data from Android tablet to iPad Pro.

2. In the following page, all items would be listed on the checkbox, including music, photos, videos, ebooks, text messages, notes, bookmarks, contacts. Check items you would like to transfer from Android to iPad Pro, and hit **Next** button

Please make sure that iPad and Android device are kept connecting with computer in the transferring process. Click **OK** when it's completed. Transfer from iPad to iPhone directly won't delete current data in the Android tablet.

Create an Apple ID

An Apple ID is the account you use to access Apple services like iCloud, the App Store, iTunes Store, Apple Books, iMessage, Apple Music, Apple TV App, or Apple Podcasts. It includes the email address and password that you use to sign in, and all the contact, payment, and security details that you'll use across Apple services. You only need one Apple ID, because you can use the same one everywhere.

If you use Apple services, you already have an Apple ID and you don't need to create a new one. No matter where you create your Apple ID, just remember to use the same one to sign in to every Apple service. That way, you can access and manage everything with a single account and password.

Create when you set up a device

When you set up on your new iPad, you might be asked to enter your Apple ID and password. If you don't have an Apple ID, you can create a new one:

- Tap Forgot password or don't have an Apple ID.
- Tap Create a Free Apple ID. You can also set it up later in Settings.
- Select your birthday and enter your name. Tap Next.
- Tap Use your current email address, or tap Get a free iCloud email address.

Use the App Store on your iPad

1. Open the App Store and tap .
2. Tap Create New Apple ID. If you don't see this option, make sure you're signed out of iCloud.
3. Enter your email, password, and choose the country or region that matches the billing address for your payment method. The email address you provide will be your new Apple ID.
4. Read the Terms and Conditions and Apple Privacy Policy, then tap Agree to Terms and Conditions. Tap Next.
5. Enter your name and birthday, then tap to subscribe to Apple Updates if you'd like. This keeps you up to date on the latest news, software, products, and services from Apple. Tap Next.
6. Enter your credit card and billing information, then tap Next. You can also choose None, and learn what to do if None isn't showing or you can't select it.

You will not be charged until you make a purchase. You can change or remove your payment details later.

7. Confirm your phone number. This can help to verify your identity and recover your account if needed. Tap Next.
8. Check your email for a verification email from Apple and follow the steps to verify your email address.

After you verify your email address, you can use your Apple ID to sign in to the iTunes Store, App Store, and other Apple services such as iCloud.

How To Sign In To iCloud With An Existing Apple ID

1. Launch the *Settings app*.
2. Tap *Sign in to your iPhone* at the top of the screen.
3. Enter the *email address and password* associated with your Apple ID.
4. Tap *Sign In*.

5. Enter your *iPhone passcode* if you have one set up.
6. Make sure your iCloud Photos are set the way you want them.
7. Toggle *Apps using iCloud* on or off, depending on your preferences.

Note: In iOS 11, you can use the Keychain password feature in the keyboard suggestion bar to add your Apple ID and password.

How To Sign Out Of iCloud On Your iPad

1. Launch the *Settings app.*
2. Tap your Apple ID at the top of the screen.
3. Scroll to the bottom and tap *Sign Out.*
4. Enter the *password* associated with your Apple ID.
5. Tap *Turn Off.*

6. Select which data you want to keep a copy of on your iPad and toggle the switch on.
7. Tap *Sign Out* in the upper right corner.
8. Tap *Sign Out* when prompted to confirm you want to sign out of iCloud on your iPad.

How To Set Up Mail, Contacts, And Calendars On iPad

No matter if you use iCloud, Gmail, or another email, calendar, or contact service, it's pretty easy to set up these on your iPad. While the old "Mail, Contacts, & Calendars" section of Settings is gone, having been split up into separate sections, there's still only one place you need to go to set up your email, contact, and calendar accounts. Here's how to setup email, contacts, and calendars on iPad.

If you're looking to set up an iCloud account on your iPad, you'll want to follow the steps here (follow these steps if you already have an Apple ID):

- Open *Settings*.
- Tap *Passwords & Accounts*.
- Tap *Add Account*.
- Tap *Google*.
- Enter your *Google account credentials*.
- Make sure the *switches* for mail, contacts, and calendars are in the 'on' or 'off' positions depending on where you want them.
- Tap *Save*.

How To Set Up Outlook.Com Mail, Calendar, And Contacts On iPad

- Open *Settings*.
- Tap *Passwords & Accounts.*
- Tap *Add Account.*

- Tap *Outlook.com*.
- Enter your *Outlook.com account credentials.*
- Tap *Yes*
- Make sure the *switches* for mail, contacts, and calendars are in the 'on' or 'off' positions depending on where you want them.
- Tap *Save*.

Setting Up Exchange Mail, Calendar, And Contacts On iPad

- Open *Settings*.
- Tap *Passwords & Accounts.*
- Tap *Add Account.*
- Tap *Exchange.*
- Enter your *Exchange email address.*
- Tap *Next*.
- Tap *Configure Manually*.

- Enter your *Exchange account information* if you elected to configure your account manually (you might need to get these from your IT administrator if you don't know them).
- Tap *Next*.
- Make sure the *switches* for mail, contacts, and calendars are in the 'on' or 'off' positions depending on where you want them.
- Tap *Save*.

How To Set Up IMAP/POP, Caldav, And Carddav On iPad

- Open *Settings*.
- Tap *Passwords & Accounts*.
- Tap *Add Account.*
- Tap *Other*.
- Select the *type* of account you want to configure. Select Mail for an email

account CalDAV for a calendar, and CardDAV for contacts.
- Enter your *account information*.
- Tap *Next*.
- Tap *Done*.

How To Adjust Display Zoom On iPad

As displays get larger, text is seemingly getting smaller. On certain iOS devices, Apple offers an option to adjust Display Zoom, which not only makes text larger, but things like the Home screen icons. Follow along to learn how to enable Display Zoom.

- Open Settings.
- Scroll down to Display & Brightness.
- Under Display Zoom, tap View. You'll now have the option to choose between Standard and Zoomed.

Note that Display Zoom is only available on iPhone 6/7/8 (Plus), iPhone XS Max, iPhone

XR, and the third-generation iPad Pro 12.9-inch.

How To Force Quit Apps On iPad Pro

In iOS 12 Apple slightly changed the method in which you access multitasking and close apps. Especially with the 2018 iPad Pros and beyond, Apple has fully adopted a gesture based navigation system that may need some time to get used to. Follow along to learn how to force quit apps on iPad Pro.

- Swipe up and hold to gain access to the multitasking interface.
- Find the app you'd like to kill.
- Swipe up on the app to kill it.

Killing apps is rather unnecessary in most scenarios. iOS manages memory well and the only real time one should consider killing an app is if it is not responding.

How to Disable Apple Music Listening History On iPhone And iPad

One of the primary benefits to disabling this feature, especially on iPad, is if you share your iPad between multiple users. This way, Apple Music suggestions don't get confused or jumbled up due to multiple users requesting music at the same time. learn how to disable this feature.

- Open the Settings app.
- Scroll down until you see Music and tap on it.
- Scroll down until you see Use Listening History.
- Switch the toggle off.

Now, when you play music through the HomePod, it will no longer use it against your listening history, giving you a better overall experience until Apple adds voice profiles.

Transfer Your Cellular Data Plan From Your Old iPad To Your New iPad

If you're picking up a new Cellular iPad to replace a current one, you have some options for transferring over your plan, depending on what kind of SIM card your iPad uses. But whether it's an embedded SIM or nano-SIM, Apple tries to make the process as painless as possible. Follow these steps to learn how go about moving your iPad cellular data plan over to your new cellular iPad.

- Open Settings on your new iPad Pro.
- Tap Cellular Data.
- Tap Set up Cellular Data.
- Tap the Transfer button if it is available.

If the transfer button doesn't appear in the Set up Cellular Data page, you might need to contact your carrier.

How To Transfer A Data Plan From One iPad With A SIM Card To Another

If you're transferring a physical SIM or nano-SIM card from your old iPad to another, here's how.

- Turn off both your old iPad and you new iPad.
- Open the SIM tray on your old iPad by using the SIM removal tool that came with your iPad.
- Remove the SIM tray from your iPad.
- Remove the SIM card from the SIM tray.
- Repeat steps 2-4 for your new iPad, though, depending on the model, it might not come with a new SIM card of its own.
- Discard the SIM card that may have come with your new iPad.
- Place the SIM card from your previous iPad into the SIM tray of your new iPad.

- Insert the SIM tray back into your new iPad, taking care to completely close the tray.
- Turn on both iPads. Activation may take a few minutes.

If the SIM cards of the two iPads are of different sizes, you'll need to contact your carrier to get a new nano-SIM to put into your new iPad. Once you get it, you'll follow the steps above, including removing the SIM from your old iPad. You just won't be moving that old SIM into your new iPad.

Use Your iPad Pro As A Display For Your Mac Mini

The folks over at Astro HQ, the developers behind Astropad, have come up with a novel use for Luna Display, the company's hardware module that turns your iPad into a full wireless touchscreen display for your Mac. By plugging Luna Display into a Mac mini and opening the Luna Display app on the new iPad

Pro, Astro HQ was able to get the iPad to serve not as a secondary display for its Mac, but a primary one.

With this setup, you can control macOS using touch and Apple Pencil, just as you would anything else on your iPad. You can also use a keyboard and mouse, as you would with any Mac.

But still, this setup was mind-blowing in other ways. There's definitely an element of inception to using your iPad as a display for your Mac. When you launch Luna, you're running your macOS on your iPad; and when you close out of the Luna app, you have a regular iPad Pro again. It's strange and exciting all at the same time, but once you settle into your workflow, it makes you wonder why this hasn't been an obvious product pairing for Apple all along.

This setup truly combines the best of both Mac and iPad, with the processing power of the Mac Mini and the edge-to-edge retina display of the iPad. Using Luna, we're able to take full advantage of every pixel on the iPad at full retina resolution. It offers more ways to interact with your macOS too, where you can seamlessly flow from mouse, to keyboard, to Apple Pencil, to touch interactions. And since Luna runs over WiFi, you have the flexibility of a completely wireless workspace. It all just works.

Of course, you don't need Apple's latest iPad Pro to do this with your own Mac mini, but with its symmetrical bezels on all four sides, it certainly makes a handsome small display for your Mac. But if you have an older iPad or iPad Pro, that should work fine, too. But no matter which iPad you use, you'll now have a touchscreen serving as your Mac's primary display, one that you can take with you all around your workspace. If you've ever wondered what it would be like to have a macOS tablet, this is the closest you'll probably get to that exact experience.

If you have Apple's new Mac mini and an iPad, you can try this out yourself. All you need is Astro's Luna Display hardware, as well as the companion app. You can find the Luna Display on the App Store for free:

As for the Luna Display hardware, it comes in two versions: USB-C and Mini DisplayPort. For the new Mac mini (and Macs released since 2016), you'll want the USB-C version.

How To Take A Screenshot With The iPad Pro

It never ceases to amaze me that taking a screenshot is so incredibly popular. Everyone does it. Whether you're grabbing a screen of your high score, want to share that funny text message thread you had with your mom, or want to ask your uncle Bob why something doesn't work right, taking a screenshot of whatever is on your device is very useful. On the iPad Pro (2018), and any device that has replaced the Home button with Face ID, there's a different method for grabbing that screenshot. Here's how.

- Navigate to the screen you want to capture.
- Set up the view exactly the way you want it for the shot.
- Press the Sleep/Wake button on the top of the iPad Pro and the Volume up button on the right side of the iPad Pro at the same time.

The screen will flash white and you will hear the sound of the camera shutter clicking (if your sound is enabled).

The screenshot will appear in the lower-left corner of the screen. Tap it to use Instant Markup to edit it before sharing it with anyone.

How To Use Instant Markup For Screenshots

You can access a screenshot you've just taken by tapping into it when it appears in the lower-left corner of the screen. This will take you to Instant Markup, which provides a number of tools for quickly editing a screenshot before saving it or sharing it.

You can crop, highlight, and mark up a screenshot. You can also add a signature, magnifier, box, and much more. When you're done, you can send it off to your friend, social media feed, or just save it in your Photo Library for future reference.

How to view and further edit screenshots

Your screenshots will automatically be saved in your Photos app.

- Open the Photos app from your Home screen.
- Tap Albums.
- Tap Screenshots.
- Select a screenshot to view or share.
- Tap Edit in the upper-right corner to edit it.

You can also tap the camera icon or use the edit menu in apps like Messages or Mail to insert your screenshot into texts, email, and more.

How To Access Instant Markup

It's easy! All you have to do is tap the little PiP (picture-in-picture) box that appears in the bottom left corner of your iPad's screen right after you take a screenshot.

If you take multiple screenshots, they will all sit in the PiP drawer. When you open Instant Markup, you can switch between screenshots.

You do, however, have to take those multiple screenshots fast. The Instant Markup PiP only sticks around for five seconds before it disappears and you have to go back into Photos to mark up your screenshots.

How To Edit A Screenshot With Instant Markup

Once you've tapped into the Instant Markup Pip, you'll see a list of tools at the bottom of the screen. You can use a marker, highlighter, pencil, eraser, or Magic Rope. Tap one of the tools to select it. You can also change the color of the writing tools from white, black, blue, green, yellow, and red.

Instant Markup lets you crop your screenshots, too. Touch and hold one of the edges or corners and drag it to the new crop.

There are four additional tools you can add to a screenshot in Instant Markup by tapping the **More** button in the bottom right corner of the screen (it looks like a plus symbol), which are:

- Add a text field - This lets you add a layer of text to your screenshot. Tap it to select the tool, then tap the newly added text field to call up the keyboard so you can write your funny quip.
- Signature - If you've already created a signature in Preview, you'll be able to add it to your screenshot from here.
- Magnifier - This is a call-out feature that will zoom in to a particular area that fits within the magnifier you've placed. You can resize and reshape the Magnifier border, and increase or decrease the amount of zoom.

- **Shapes** - You can add a particular shape to your screenshot from square, circle, speech bubble, and arrow. You can either have a solid or outlined shape, and you can adjust its size and shape by dragging the edges.

If you make a mistake, you can undo each previous step by tapping the undo button in the bottom left of the screen. Conversely, you can redo any steps by tapping the redo button in the same location.

How To Save An Edited Screenshot From Instant Markup

Screenshots that have been edited with Markup will not automatically be saved to your Photo library. You'll want to save them before you close Instant Markdown.

- Tap **Done** in the upper left corner of Instant Markup.
- Select **Save to Photos**.

- Alternatively, you could select **Delete Screenshot** if you want to delete the marked up screenshot.
- Tap **Done**, then tap **Save** or **Delete**

How To Share An Edited Screenshot From Instant Markup

Once you've annotated the bah-jeesus out of your screenshot, you can share it using the Share feature in iOS. It works the same way that sharing documents and other media work across iOS.

- Tap the **Share** icon in the upper right corner of the Instant Markup screen.
- Select how you want to share the screenshot.
- Fill out the appropriate contact information or status update and send it.
- Tap **Share**, then select where to share the screenshot

How To Disable Instant Markup

At this time, you can't disable Instant Markup. While I know I'm going to love having this feature, I can see it being a bother for some people. Hopefully, Apple will update iOS with the ability to disable Instant Markup soon.

iPad Pencil

Which Apple Pencil works with your iPad? If you have an iPad Pro 11-inch or iPad Pro 12.9-inch (3rd generation), you can use Apple Pencil (2nd generation). You cannot use the original Apple Pencil with these iPad models.

If you have one of these iPad models, you can use the original Apple Pencil:

- iPad Pro 12.9-inch (1st or 2nd generation)
- iPad Pro 10.5-inch

- iPad Pro 9.7-inch
- iPad (6th generation)

You cannot use Apple Pencil (2nd generation) with these iPad models.

Pair Your Apple Pencil With Your iPad

The first time you use your Apple Pencil, you have to pair it with your iPad. If you have an iPad Pro 11-inch or iPad Pro 12.9-inch (3rd generation), attach your Apple Pencil to the magnetic connector on the side of your iPad Pro.

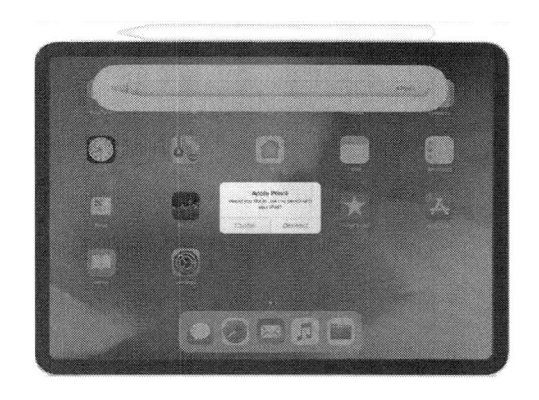

If you have one of these models, remove the cap from your Apple Pencil and plug it into the Lightning connector on your iPad:

- iPad Pro 12.9-inch (1st or 2nd generation)
- iPad Pro 10.5-inch
- iPad Pro 9.7-inch
- iPad (6th generation)

When you see the Pair button, tap it.

After you pair your Apple Pencil, it will stay paired until you restart your iPad, turn on airplane mode, or pair with another iPad. Just pair your Apple Pencil again when you're ready to use it.

How To Use Apple Pencil

You can use Apple Pencil to write, markup, and draw with built-in apps and apps from the

App Store. With some apps, like Notes, you can draw and sketch with an Apple Pencil. To draw or sketch in the Notes app:

- Open Notes.
- Tap
- To draw, tap ⒶIf you don't see Ⓐ, upgrade your notes. To sketch, tap ⊕, then tap Add Sketch.
- Start your drawing or sketch. You can choose from several drawing tools and colors, and switch to the eraser if you make a mistake. When you draw or sketch, you can tilt your Apple Pencil to shade a line and press more firmly to darken the line.

If you draw near the edge of the screen with your Apple Pencil, iOS won't activate Control Center, Notification Center, or Multitasking.

You can draw anywhere on the screen without getting interrupted.

With iPad Pro 11-inch and iPad Pro 12.9-inch (3rd generation), you can double-tap the lower section of Apple Pencil to quickly switch back to the tool you used last. You can change what happens when you double-tap your Apple Pencil by going to Settings > Apple Pencil. Choose between these:

- Switch between current tool and eraser
- Switch between current tool and last used
- Show color palette
- Off

Double-tap only works in supported apps, like Notes.

Charge Your Apple Pencil

For iPad Pro 11-inch and iPad Pro 12.9-inch (3rd generation): To charge, make sure that Bluetooth is turned on for your iPad. Then attach your Apple Pencil to the magnetic connector at the center of the right side of your iPad.

For iPad Pro 12.9-inch (1st or 2nd generation), iPad Pro 10.5-inch, iPad Pro 9.7-inch, and iPad (6th generation): To charge, plug your Apple Pencil into the Lightning connector on your iPad. You can also charge it with a USB Power Adapter by using the Apple Pencil Charging Adapter that came with your Apple Pencil. Apple Pencil will fast charge when plugged into either power source. To see how much charge your Apple Pencil has left, check the Widgets view on your iPad.

If your Apple Pencil won't pair with your iPad:

- Make sure to center your Apple Pencil on the magnetic connector on the right edge of the iPad.
- Restart your iPad, then try to pair again.
- Go to Settings > Bluetooth and make sure that Bluetooth is turned on.
- On the same screen, look under My Devices for your Apple Pencil. If you see it, tap . Then tap Forget this Device.
- Connect your Apple Pencil in to your iPad and tap the Pair button when it appears after a few seconds.
- If you don't see the Pair button, wait for one minute while your Apple Pencil charges. Then try connecting your Apple Pencil again and wait until you see the Pair button.
- If you still don't see the Pair button, contact Apple Support.

How To Scan, Sign, And Send Documents

There are few tasks more agonizing than trying to quickly scan, sign, and send documents. In this day and age, it should be easy — but without a tablet, it can be frustrating booting up your scanner, opening that inadequate trial version of Adobe Reader gathering dust on your desktop, and woefully using a mouse or trackpad to sign on the dotted line with all the grace and elegance of a toddler who has yet to develop fine motor skills.

Thankfully, if you own an iPad Pro, firing off official documents is a snap, one that takes a fraction of the time you'd spend fighting with your PC. Simply open the **Notes** app, tap the **addition sign** in the bottom-right corner, select **Scan Documents**, and take a picture of the paper. Your iPad will then convert the document into a clear, crisp PDF that you can sign with your Apple Pencil.

How To Create, Customize, And Use Memoji In iOS 12

The brand-spanking new iOS 12 packs in a ton of new features, but one of my favorites is Memoji, which expands on Animojis, which were introduced last year. Rather than interacting as an animal, alien, or poop emoji, you can now send a customized Animoji that looks exactly like you.

Animoji was originally only available for the iPhone X thanks to its TrueDepth camera, but that's not the case anymore following the announcement of Apple's new lineup of iPhones — the iPhone XS, iPhone XS Max, and iPhone XR. Since all four iPhone devices now have the same camera technology, you can now create and send Animojis and Memojis to more people than ever.

After downloading iOS 12, we decided to test out the Memoji feature by creating our own. Aside from the extremely simple process, we enjoyed all the different customization options — from pink hair to blue skin, Memoji lets your imagination run wild. Its accuracy wasn't only apparent in the way it physically looked either — we also enjoyed how quickly and realistically it picked up on our facial expressions. Here is how to create and use Memoji.

HOW TO CREATE YOUR MEMOJI

To create your Memoji, you have to head into **iMessage** and open a new or existing conversation. Once you open your **App Drawer** and select the **Animoji icon**, swipe all the way to the right until you reach "**New Memoji**" and tap the **plus sign** icon.

You will then be able to customize your Memoji based on a variety of physical features. Apple offers a multitude of options to make your avatar as unique as possible — like the ability to add freckles and choose from a wide range of skin tones and hair colors. You can also alter your head shape, eyebrows, nose, lips, ears, and more.

Aside from physical traits, you can also dress up your Memoji. There are plenty of hats, headpieces, and eyewear to choose from that are also customizable by color. Under the ear section, you can also choose from a variety of earrings — hoops or studs.

Once you are done creating your Memoji, all you have to do is tap "**Done**" in the upper-right-hand corner. It will then live in the gallery alongside the other Animojis in the drawer. If you ever want to switch the way your Memoji looks, tap on the icon with the three dots in the lower left-hand corner and choose "**Edit**." You will then be brought back to the same customization options as before to make your changes. If you want to have multiple versions of your Memoji available without having to constantly edit it, you can also choose the "**Duplicate**" option.

HOW TO USE YOUR MEMOJI

To use your Memoji, open the **App Drawer** while in the iMessage window, select the **Animoji icon**, and swipe through to find your Memoji. Since your Memoji mirrors your muscle movements, you want to make sure your face is in view of the camera. Once you're ready, tap the record button in the lower left-hand corner. As part of the new update, Apple extended the amount of time you have to record your Animoji — rather than 10 seconds, you now have 30 seconds.

Once you're done, you can tap on the record button again to end it — but it will only appear if you haven't used the full 30 seconds. You will then be able to watch it playback once, and can choose to watch it again by tapping on Replay above your Memoji. If you're not satisfied, you can tap on the garbage can icon to delete it and try again. To send it, simply tap the blue arrow — the recipient will then be able to play it from their iMessage window once it's delivered, but you can choose to replay it as well by tapping on it in the message window.

You can also add your Memoji into photos you take through the camera in iMessage. Once the front-facing camera is open, you can overlay your Memoji onto your own head, snap the photo, and send it. The same goes for FaceTime — while video chatting with someone else, you can apply the Memoji to live video.

HOW IT STACKS UP AGAINST THE COMPETITION

Even though Memoiji is the first of its kind for Apple, custom avatars aren't new. In March, Samsung launched AR Emoji — available in the Galaxy S9 and S9 Plus — which had mixed reviews. Rather than customizing it from the beginning the way you do with Memoji, AR Emoji creates the foundation for you using your selfie. You're then able to alter it based on skin tone, hair color, eye color, and outfit.

Apple's new feature can also be compared to Bitmoji — which doesn't mirror facial expressions but can be used to create an avatar that looks exactly like you. Aside from the fact that you're able to use it across all platforms and devices (rather than being restricted to the iPhone X lineup or Samsung Galaxy S9), there are also deeper customization options. As part of its update in February, Bitmoji Deluxe allows users to alter anything from different hair treatments to minor details like wrinkles on the forehead, cheeks, or eyes — which resulted in us taking hours to create our Bitmoji.

With Memoji, we found the feature had the right amount of customization and enjoyed creating it. The process is not only simple, but there are enough choices to make us feel content with the way it looks (without having to over think it) and excited to actually send it out to people. We also appreciate the attention to detail in not only accurately capturing our facial expressions, but the way our hair also swayed from side to side when we moved our head even slightly.

The entire Animoji family currently consists of only talking heads, and we do wish Memojis had bodies to go along with the heads. When using AR Emoji and Bitmoji, we're able to express a bit more through hand gestures, which makes our avatars look that much more lively and fun. Plus, it would also be nice to have the option to customize outfits in addition to facial features.

Apple Pay

Apple Pay, which lives inside the Wallet app, keeps all your credit cards, debit cards, store cards, and loyalty cards safe and secure on your iPhone or iPad. With Apple Pay you can use your Visa, Mastercard, American Express card, or Discover Card at any store that accepts tap-to-pay, or in any app that incorporates it. With Wallet, you can also board a plane, scan for your coffee, get into a movie or concert, accumulate loyalty points, and more. All right from your lock screen or with the tap of an icon.

How to Manage Apple Pay

Buying with Apple Pay is incredibly convenient, but it's even more convenient if things like your shipping address are properly set up and ready for you in advance. Once you've made the purchase, being able to see your transactions, both recent and detailed, means never having to wonder about a purchase or wait for a statement again.

How to Use Wallet

Wallet— formerly known as Passbook — is Apple's digital answer to manage the cards that are overfilling your purse, wallet, and pockets. Location aware, Wallet can conveniently present appropriate cards for you right on the lock screen whenever you get close to your coffee shop or airport. Always connected, Wallet can even update your balance or gate number in real time so you always know how much you have or where you need to be.

How To Set up 'Hey Siri' on iPad

When you set up a new iPhone or iPad, you'll be asked if you want to use "Hey Siri!" voice activation. If you do, you'll be walked through the set up. If you don't, you can change your mind and turn it on at any time in Settings. Here's how!

- Launch *Settings* from your Home screen.
- Tap on *Siri & Search*
- Tap the *Listen for "Hey Siri* switch to turn it on.

How to Train "Hey Siri" to Your Voice

Whether part of the set up process or later, as soon as you turn on "Hey Siri", you'll need to train it to recognize your voice.

- Tap *Set Up Now*.
- Say *Hey Siri!* When prompted.
- Say *Hey Siri!* Again when prompted.
- Say *Hey Siri!* One more time when prompted.
- Say *Hey Siri, how's the weather?* When prompted.
- Say *Hey Siri, it's me!* When prompted.
- Tap *Done*.

Now, "Hey Siri" will activate — but only if it sounds like your voice.

How to Use "Hey Siri!"

"Hey Siri!" is, by design, ridiculously easy to use. You literally just say, "Hey Siri" to initiate the start of your interaction.

- Position yourself within audio range of your iPhone or iPad
- Say "Hey Siri!" loud enough for your iPhone or iPad to hear you.
- Tell Siri what you want it to do — "call mom on speaker", "make a dinner reservation", "what's the weather like in Bermuda?", etc.

How Secure Is "Hey Siri!" Voice ID?

We've tested "Hey Siri!" with over a half-dozen voices and nothing has worked except the registered voice or a recording of the registered voice, but that can vary. But Voice ID on Hey Siri isn't meant for security. Don't mistake it for "My voice is my passport, authorize me!" It's meant to solve the problem of unintentional activation, be it accidental, prank, or malicious.

If you're worried about security, turn "Hey Siri" off and stick with manual activation. If you're interested in the convenience of voice activation while you're caring for children, cooking, working, or otherwise have you hands full, then know the limitations but enjoy the functionality.

Troubleshoot Common Problems

The iPad Pro's 12.9-inch display, split-screen support, and 10-hour battery life are tempting millions into buying Apple's biggest tablet ever. It's an attractive device for productivity and creativity, but it's not flawless. If you've recently splurged on one, then you have every right to expect it to work perfectly. Unfortunately, for some people it has been behaving unprofessionally. These are the most common iPad Pro problems currently being reported, with advice on how you should work around them, or, if possible, fix them.

iPad Pro shuts down or restarts by itself

We've seen quite a few threads in the Apple support forums about the iPad Pro shutting down by itself or randomly restarting for no apparent reason.

Possible solutions:

- Hold down the Sleep/Wake and Home buttons together for at least 10 seconds, or until you see the Apple logo. This may at least temporarily fix the issue.
- If you notice that crashes occur when you are using a specific app or playing a specific game, then try uninstalling it and test to see if the problem is gone.
- Back up your data, then try a factory reset. Restore your backup when it's

done and test to see if the problem returns. If it does, then you might consider a factory reset followed by setting up the iPad Pro as a new device, instead of restoring the backup. It's possible that one of the apps you've installed or something in your settings is causing the crashes, so setting up as new could help. Just be vigilant when you do start reinstalling apps for anything that seems to introduce a problem.
- If the problem persists after you've factory reset and set up the device as new, then you need to contact Apple.

Echo in Skype calls and other video calls

A lot of people have found that callers on the other end of video calls when using the iPad Pro are hearing an echo. It doesn't happen with FaceTime, but it does happen with a number of third-party apps such as Skype and Facebook Messenger. This problem has been reported several times on the Apple support forums and on Microsoft's forum.

Workaround:

- If you have a headset or earphones with a microphone, you can plug them in and the echo will be gone.

Possible solution:

- This looks to be a software issue. The fact that FaceTime doesn't suffer from the problem suggests that the developers of other video calls apps may be able to update their software to fix it. It may be worth uninstalling the app you're having a problem with, turning off your iPad Pro, turning it back on, and then reinstalling the app.

- Take a look in Settings > General > Software Update to make sure your iPad Pro has the latest software from Apple.
- If the problem persists then contact the developer of the app you're having problems with and report it. You should also report it to Apple.

Can't connect to Wi-Fi

A few people are having trouble getting the iPad Pro to connect to a Wi-Fi network, while others are experiencing poor internet connectivity and interference. This is a very common issue for all sorts of devices, and it's usually fairly easy to fix. Here's what to try:

Possible solutions:

- Turn your router and your iPad Pro off and on again. Hold down the Sleep/Wake and Home buttons together for around

10 seconds and you should see the Apple logo as the device reboots. It's also worth restarting the router if you can.

- Try resetting all your network settings by going to Settings > General > Reset > Reset Network Settings. You'll have to input your passwords again.
- If your router has MAC filtering turned on, then you may need to turn it off. It is possible to add your iPad's MAC address, but due to Apple's MAC randomization, there's a good chance it's going to change and refuse to connect the next time you try. The simplest solution is just to turn MAC filtering off altogether.
- It's possible that your DNS settings are the problem. You can change them in Settings > Wi-Fi by tapping the "i" icon next to your network and scrolling down to DNS. Tap on the numbers and change

them to "8.8.8.8" or "8.8.8.4" if you want to use Google's servers, or you could use OpenDNS, which is "208.67.222.222" or "208.67.222.220".

- If you're using a VPN service, make sure you have the latest updates.
- Make sure that your router firmware is fully updated. You may need to check with your ISP or the router manufacturer.
- If you believe you're experiencing interference, considering moving your router to a new location. A wall (or several walls) would be causing interference between your iPad and the router.

Screen freezing during use

Some people have found that the iPad Pro keeps freezing while in use, with people stating it can freeze during startup or when using apps. The screen will freeze and can remain unresponsive for a number of seconds. It may resume as normal, or stay frozen indefinitely.

Workaround:

- Try double clicking the Home button to bring up the app switcher screen and swipe to close the app you were using when the screen froze. This seems to temporarily fix the problem for some people, but others report that the touchscreen is still unresponsive when they exit the app switcher screen.
- Hold down the Sleep/Wake and Home buttons together for at least 10 seconds, or until you see the Apple logo. Your iPad Pro should work again now, but the problem might crop up again.

Possible fixes:

- You can try resetting all of the device's settings by going to Settings > General > Reset > Reset All Settings.
- You should try restoring your iPad Pro to factory settings via iTunes. Back up any precious files first, then plug your iPad Pro into your computer using the cable that came with it. Launch iTunes and choose your iPad Pro, then click on Summary and Restore. Click Restore again to confirm. Keep in mind that restoring from a backup may reintroduce the problem, though, you could try testing for a while without restoring a backup to see if the issue is resolved.
- If the problem persists, even after a restore with a fresh set up and without restoring a backup, then it's time to contact Apple or take your iPad Pro into the nearest Apple Store and ask about a replacement.

Battery life is poor

There is a whopping 10,307 mAh battery in the 12.9-inch iPad Pro, and a 7,306 mAh battery in the smaller 9.7-inch iPad Pro. Both should keep you going for ten hours at a time, but not everyone is finding the battery life to be as advertised, with some noticing a drain while the device is plugged in and charging. If you find that the battery is draining much faster than expected, especially if it's draining quickly while in standby, you may have a problem.

Workarounds:

- With a 12.9-inch screen to power, brightness will have a big impact on the iPad Pro's battery. Go to Settings > Display & Brightness and turn the brightness down. Set a comfortable level and then enable Auto-Brightness to

cater for different background lighting situations.
- If you have a lot of apps refreshing content in the background it can really drain your battery. Go to Settings > General > Background App Refresh and toggle off any apps you don't need updating themselves. They'll still refresh when you open them.

Possible solutions:

- It's always worth trying a simple restart. Hold down the Sleep/Wake button and swipe slide to power off, then turn it on again. You could also hold down the Sleep/Wake and Home buttons together, until you see the Apple logo, to force a reboot.
- If the drain only occurs when it's charged, consider leaving the iPad Pro to charge completely before using it again.

Heavy use of the iPad while it's charging could be using more power than it can replenish.

- Go to Settings > Battery and look under Battery Usage. If there's a problem app, make sure that it's fully updated. If that doesn't help, you may want to try uninstalling it and see if you can find a replacement.
- A factory reset could solve your problem. Back up everything on your iPad and go to Settings > General > Reset > Erase All Content and Settings to try it. Try testing the battery life before you restore a backup.
- If battery life is still bad after a factory reset, then it's time to contact Apple.

Smart Keyboard not working

Quite a few reports have popped up about the Smart Keyboard failing to work properly after waking up from sleep. For some, shortcuts like Command and Tab, which would usually cycle through apps, no longer work. On further examination it seems this problem can occur on any hardware keyboard connected to the iPad Pro.

Workarounds:

- If you detach and then reattach the keyboard, it may start working again, but the problem can come back.
- Restarting the iPad Pro will also bring back functionality temporarily.

Possible solutions:

- Check the port that connects the smart keyboard to the iPad Pro for debris or damage. Clean out any debris, or seek repairs if the port appears damaged.

- iOS 10.2.1 contains a number of bug fixes. One fix may alleviate the smart keyboard issue.

Unable to view and play videos

There are multiple threads on the Apple Discussion forums containing people who are having trouble watching videos from various places on their iPad Pro. Some are unable to watch their own personal movies, while others can't watch videos from streaming services like YouTube.

Possible solutions:

- Restart the iPad by pressing and holding the Home and Sleep/Wake buttons until the Apple logo appears.
- iOS 10.2 has been said to be the culprit behind this problem, if you haven't update to iOS 10.2.1, which includes various bug fixes, do so.

- Apple Discussion forums user Savage1969 has a potential fix that involves pretending to buy something from iTunes to get your video library to appear:
    - Open the TV app, then tap Store.
    - Scroll to the bottom of the page and tap Free Episodes. Pick anything you wish by tapping Get, but you don't have to actually download it.
    - Go back to the TV app, and tap Library in the bottom row.
    - Tap Library, located in the top left corner of the screen, then tap Home Videos.
- Perform a factory reset and restore the iPad from a backup or as a new device.

Apple Pencil battery widget   disappears

Several iPad Pro owners have noticed the disappearance of the battery widget that lets them know their Apple Pencil has been connected, and informs them of the device's remaining battery life. This is especially annoying for those that don't want their pencil to stop working during use because they were unaware of its battery level.

Possible solutions:

- Restart the iPad Pro.
- Go to Settings > Bluetooth and make sure Bluetooth is on. Make sure the Apple Pencil appears on this screen as well.
- User VermillionPixel provided the following steps that other users found to be helpful:
    - Unpair the Apple Pencil from the iPad Pro by going to Settings >

Bluetooth > My Devices > the blue "i" icon > Forget this Device, then restart the iPad.
- When the iPad Pro is on again, connect the pencil to the iPad using the Lightning connector. Accept the pairing request, then disconnect the pencil. The battery widget should appear again.

No app or system sounds

Some owners are missing the sounds that typically play when using the iPad Pro, such as the app sounds and general system sounds like Keyboard and Lock clicks.

Possible solutions:

- Swipe up from the bottom of the screen to open the Control Center. If the bell symbol/Mute is on/white, tap it to turn it off.

- If your Keyboard and Lock sounds are missing, go to Settings > Sounds, then scroll to the bottom and tap the toggles next to Keyboard Clicks and Lock Sounds. On this same page, adjust the Ringers and Alerts slider at the top of the page.

I believe this book has been able to help you to master your iPad device. I want to thank you for purchasing this book. God bless you!

Books By The Author

Made in the USA
Middletown, DE
15 January 2019